Anonymous

California

Commission for examining voting machines. Report to the senate and

assembly, 33rd session of the legislature.

Anonymous

California

Commission for examining voting machines. Report to the senate and assembly, 33rd session of the legislature.

ISBN/EAN: 9783744726368

Printed in Europe, USA, Canada, Australia, Japan

Cover: Foto ©Suzi / pixelio.de

More available books at **www.hansebooks.com**

REPORT OF THE COMMISSION

FOR THE PURPOSE OF

Examining, Testing and Investigating
VOTING MACHINES

TO THE

SENATE AND ASSEMBLY

THIRTY-THIRD SESSION OF THE LEGISLATURE

OF THE

STATE OF CALIFORNIA.

OAKLAND
ENQUIRER PUBLISHING COMPANY
1898

To the Senate and Assembly of the Thirty-third Session of the Legislature of the State of California:

IN compliance with an Act—(see Appendix "A")—passed at the last session of the Legislature—approved March 27, 1897,—creating a Commission for the purpose of examining, testing and investigating Voting Machines, the undersigned were duly appointed Commissioners by the Governor. On May 21, 1897, this Commission met in San Francisco and organized by the election of W. M. Hinton as president and C. B. Morgan as secretary. An office was engaged in the Central Bank Building, Oakland, and regular meetings were ordered to be held on the first and third Saturdays in each month. Notice of the organization of the Commission, the time and place of meeting, and the purpose for which it was created, was given to the Associated Press and generally published in the newspapers. Special notice was given, from time to time, by letter containing a copy of the Act creating the Commission, to the following named Inventors and those interested in Voting Machines:

DATE.	NAME.	ADDRESS.
May 25, 1897	Hamilton Kibbie	Oblong, Ill.
May 25, 1897	F. X. St. Louis	Elk Creek P. O., Glenn Co., Cal.
June 5, 1897	A. O. Abbott	Hudson, Mich.
June 5, 1897	John Blocher	Franklin Grove, Ill.
June 5, 1897	S. Aronson	Brooklyn, N. Y.
June 5, 1897	Geo. A Cline	Toronto, Canada
June 5, 1897	E. H. Davis	Elmira, N. Y.
June 7, 1897	D. Dobbins	Franklin, Ind.
June 7, 1897	S. E. Davis	Rochester, N. Y.
June 7, 1897	W. W. Ford	Longview, Tex.
June 7, 1897	A. J. Gillespie	Atlantic, Iowa
June 7, 1897	F. H. Gilbert	Ridgefield, Wash.
June 9, 1897	C. Christensen	1115 10th Ave., East Oakland

DATE.	NAME.	ADDRESS.
June 9, 1897	Wm. H. Honiss	Hartford, Conn.
June 5, 1897	L. S. Harmsen	Minneapolis, Minn.
June 9, 1897	L. Y. McConnell	Rochester, N. Y.
June 9, 1897	J. H. Myers	Rochester, N. Y,
June 9, 1897	P. S. McGee	Dodgeville, Mass.
June 9, 1897	J. H. McTammany	Spencer, Mass.
June 5, 1897	C. F. Roper	Hopedale, Mass.
June 9, 1897	C. A. Stitzer	Central City, Neb.
June 9, 1897	J. H. Scotford	Portland, Or.
June 9, 1897	Geo. W. Trahan	Howena, La.
June 10, 1897	F. C. Moseback	522 Montgomery St., S. F.
June 10, 1897	C. E. Stanton	Santa Ana, Orange Co., Cal.
June 12, 1897	G. E. Kennedy	Livermore, Cal.
June 12, 1897	J. B. Clot	San Franciso, Cal.
June 12, 1897	S. Ducas	San Francisco, Cal.
June 12, 1897	H. A. Clifford	San Francisco, Cal.
June 12, 1897	J. Mourot	Modesto, Cal.
June 12, 1897	T. D. Strong	San Francisco, Cal.
June 12, 1897	J. G. Sweeney	Petaluma, Cal.
June 14, 1897	Dr. A. Grim	Franklin Grove, Ill.
June 16, 1897	Daniel Davis	115 E. Henry St., Elmira, N. Y.
June 16, 1897	A. S. Hamilton	Rochester, N. Y.
Aug. 27, 1897	A. B. Foster	Oakland, Cal.
Sept. 8, 1897	C. L. Sturges	Escondido, Cal.
Sept. 30, 1897	Wm. R. Pike	St. Paul, Minn.
Oct. 2, 1897	Henry Weber	N. Temescal, Cal.
Oct. 20, 1897	Lorenzo J. Markoo	White Bear, Minn.
Oct. 20, 1897	Henry H. Niebur	Ferndale, Cal.
Oct. 20, 1897	Edwin B. Olmstead	Delevan, N. Y.
Oct. 20, 1897	Edwin G. Richards	Sharon, Mass.
Oct. 20, 1897	Enoch H. Towne	Worcester, Mass.
Oct. 20, 1897	Rhines Ballot System Co.	St. Paul, Minn.
Oct. 20, 1897	Clinton L. Bancroft	Browns, Humboldt Co, Cal.
Oct. 20, 1897	A. C. Beranck	Chicago, Ill.
Oct. 20, 1897	Jas. G. H. Buck	Dallas, Tex.
Oct. 20, 1897	Edwin B. Cummings	Indianapolis, Ind.
Oct. 20, 1897	Wm. M. Cutter	Marysville, Cal.
Oct. 20, 1897	Montana Vote Registering. Machine Co	Missoula, Mont.
Oct. 20, 1897	Thos. G. Ferguson	Colby, Kas.
Oct. 20, 1897	Jas. G. Hardy, Jr	Canton, N. Y.
Oct. 20, 1897	R. A. Hart	Battle Creek, Mich.
Dec. 11, 1897	Davis Voting Machine Co	New York, N. Y.
Dec. 11, 1897	Clarence A. Evans	Upland, Penn.
Dec. 11, 1897	U. S. Voting Machine Co.	Jamestown, N. Y.
Dec. 11, 1897	George M. Greer	McCool Junction, Neb.

DATE.	NAME.	ADDRESS.

Dec. 11, 1897..Chas. R. Rofer .... Hopedale, Mass.
Jan. 13, 1898..Clement de Croes .... Westport, Ind.
Jan. 13, 1898...Jas. J. Cunningham and
      Eugene H. Mullen.....Lynn, Mass.
Mar. 18, 1897..Turner Voting Machine Co.Indianapolis, Ind.
June 24, 1898..John K. Hogan........ ...Placerville, Cal.
July 21, 1898..A. J. Bolfing............. San Francisco, Cal.
Aug. 15, 1898..Albert Suoock............ Hartford, Conn.

And responses, in person or by letter, were received from:

Hamilton Kibbie........ Oblong, Ill.
F. X. St. Louis........... Elk Creek P. O., Glenn Co., Cal.
A. C. Abbott .... Hudson, Mich.
E. H. Davis............... Elmira, N. Y.
A. J. Gillespie............ Atlantic, Iowa.
F. H. Gilbert............. Ridgefield, Wash.
C. Christensen........... 1115 10th Ave., E. Oakland, Cal.
Wm. H. Honiss........... Hartford, Conn.
J. H. Myers .... Rochester, N. Y.
J. H. McTammany........ Spencer, Mass.
P. C. Moseback........... 522 Montgomery St., S. F.
C. E. Stanton............ Santa Ana, Orange Co., Cal.
G. E. Kennedy........... Livermore, Cal.
H. A. Clifford............ San Francisco, Cal.
J. Mourot................ Modesto, Cal.
J. G. Sweeney............ Petaluma, Cal.
Dr. A. Grim............. Franklin Grove, Ill.
Daniel Davis............. 115 E. Henry St., Elmira, N. Y.
A. B. Foster............. Oakland, Cal.
C. L. Sturges............. Escondido, Cal.
Wm. R. Pike .... St. Paul, Minn.
Henry Weber............. N. Temescal, Cal.
Henry H. Niebur......... Ferndale, Cal.
Edwin B. Olmstead......... Delevan, N. Y.
Clinton L. Bancroft....... Browns, Humboldt Co., Cal
Edwin B. Cummings...... Indianapolis, Ind.
Thos. G. Ferguson........ Colby, Kas.
Davis Voting Machine Co..New York, N. Y.
Clarence A. Evans........ Upland, Penn.
Clement de Croes......... Westport, Ind.
Cunningham & Mullen....Lynn, Mass.
Turner Voting Machine Co.Indianapolis, Ind.
J. C. Garrett.............. San Francisco, Cal.
Jap Jones................ Oakland, Cal.

Jeff Kindleberger..........San Francisco, Cal.
Standard Voting Machine
    Co................... ..Rochester, N. Y.
S. A. Crumrine............Los Angeles, Cal.
A. J. Bolfing..............San Francisco, Cal.

The question whether a provision for independent voting was a necessary legal requirement arose early in our investigations.   In order to obtain light upon this subject the secretary was, on July 3, 1897, directed to address the Attorney-General upon the subject, and reference is hereby made to Appendix " B " for the correspondence which ensued.

Article 2, Section 1197, of the Political Code provides:— " There shall be left at the end of the list of candidates for each office as many blank spaces as there are persons to be elected to such office, in which the voter may insert the name of any person not printed upon the ballot for whom he desires to vote as candidates for such office, and the name and blank spaces on the whole ticket shall be consecutively numbered." Whether this be merely a Legislative provision or a Constitutional requirement, it can be maintained, and modified so as to be adapted to Machine Voting.

The additional mechanism required to permit a voter to exercise such a privilege or right, of necessity, adds to the cost of a machine and complicates its movements and prolongs the time required in canvassing the result at the close of the poll.   Machines without such attachments will show the results of the poll as rapidly as they can be read.   If, however, an election should be contested on the ground that any voter had been denied a constitutional right in consequence of no provision having been made for independent voting, and such contest should be sustained by the Supreme Court, the investment in such machines would be lost.   This would involve the loss of large sums of money and is a risk which can be avoided by the adoption of a machine which provides for independent voting.   Some machines which are provided with an attachment for independent voting preserve secrecy better than the present ballot system, as the independent vote cannot be associated with the votes cast for regular nominees.   Under the present ballot system any ballot can be readily dentified by the voter and his patron arranging for a given name to be written upon a given blank space (see Sec. 1197 Art. II) and the secrecy of the ballot be destroyed.

The newly adopted charter of San Francisco provides for the election of eighteen Supervisors, to be elected at large, at each election. Under the present ballot system eighteen blank spaces would be provided for a voter to write in such names as he might desire, and any attempt on the part of a voter to vote repeatedly for the same person would be apparent and such repeated votes, under existing law, would not be counted. If no check is provided against cumulative voting in the attachment for independent voting on a machine, the door would be opened to favor unnominated candidates over those regularly nominated. Thus: Eighteen votes for Supervisor could be given by one voter to the man of his choice while those regularly nominated could receive but one vote from each voter, except on such machines as designedly permit of cumulative voting. It becomes, therefore, of vital importance that any device for independent voting must detect and, unless permitted, prevent cumulative voting.

In order to permit a voter to write the name of any person not printed upon the ticket for whom he desires to vote, the inventors of voting machines have resorted to several systems. Amongst these may be mentioned—First: The dual system of machine and ballot box voting, which affords the voter the option of voting by either method and which necessitates the adding together of the results of each to obtain the total vote for each candidate; Second : A device to permit the voter to deposit some kind of a ballot within the machine ; Third : A recording scroll attached to the machine upon which a voter can write, but confining all such votes to a lineal space for each voter so as to detect repeating.

The first system presents no improvement upon the present ballot system and would only tend to complicate it. The second offers little, if any, advantage over the first, as the count of the ballots would have to be added to the results shown upon the machines in order to obtain the total vote of each candidate.

If only one ballot was employed upon which the names of all candidates voted for would have to be written, such ballot could readily be identified by writing an agreed name upon it. The same objection would apply if but one ballot for co-ordinate offices should be used. In both those cases voters who might desire to vote for, say, seventeen regularly nominated candidates for Supervisor and one not nominated, would be obliged to write the names of the eighteen and would thus be subjected "to casting their votes upon more burdensome conditions than are imposed upon others no better entitled under the fundamental law to the free and untrammeled exercise of the right of suffrage." (Eaton vs. Brown 96 Cal.) On the other hand, if ballots upon which only one name could be written were used, it would be necessary, in order to detect cumulative voting, to have all ballots used by one voter numbered alike. Such ballots would necessarily have to be small and for the purpose of canvassing would have to be segregated and placed in line. Should a large number of such ballots be cast (for instance for eighteen Supervisors) the system would prove impractical and be exposed to fraud by substituting prepared ballots for those cast by the voters.

The third system will show at the close of the polls an immediate and complete return of the votes cast for all regularly nominated candidates whose names appear printed upon the ballots attached to the machines, and from the nature of the case the independent vote must be counted separately as no one can foresee how many or for whom such votes will be cast.

In this connection it is to be borne in mind that any voting system is like a chain—its weakest link is the measure of its strength. In the past, independent voting (aside from its use to identify a ballot) has offered no opportunity for abuse, but if in providing for independent voting in connection with machine voting an opportunity is opened for fraud, it is safe to predict that this fraudulent method of voting will be largely developed.

Inventors in designing voting machines, as a rule, have adopted one of two plans, i. e., First : The arrangement of parties at right angles to the offices to be filled, thus :

	Rep.	Dem.	Pop.	Social	Ind.	Irregular.
Mayor						
Auditor...............						
Treasurer.............						
City Attorney......						
City Engineer.......						

or the reverse arrangement—and

Second : The arrangement of candidates in groups for the same office, practically as they are now printed upon the ballots under the existing law. By the first plan an increase in the number of parties or independent candidates in excess of the columns established upon the machine would render such machine useless for the purpose of conducting an election. In view of the tendency to increase in the number of parties this becomes a matter of much importance, as an increase in the number of parties in excess of the capacity of a Machine would block an election.

The second plan permits an increase in the number of parties and candidates by coupling machines together until all candidates have been accommodated.

Under the first plan the following machines have been designed :

McTammany.

Standard Voting Machine Co.

H. H. Niebur.

U. S. Ballot Box.

And under the second plan are the following :

California Voting Machine Co.

Christ Christensen.

Ellis Ballot Machine Co.

National Voting Machine.

In designing Voting Machines, inventors have in many cases arranged for the casting of an entire party vote by the movement of one key, simultaneously locking all others. Under the decision of the Supreme Court of this State in Easton vs. Brown, California Reports 96, folio 371, "Voters can only express their choice by placing a stamp opposite the name of their candidate for each office or by writing the name of a candidate in a blank space left therefor or their answer to each question or proposition or proposed amendment to the Constitution, except only in case of presidential electors, who may under the law be voted for in groups by a single impression of the stamp.''

The above ruling applied to a voting machine would render mechanisms for casting a party vote by the operation of one key superfluous, and such mechanisms if retained would only tend to confuse a voter. Machines designed for candidates for the same office to be grouped together and for all candidates to be voted for separately, correspond with the existing law and rulings in this State—the provision in the case of presidential electors excepted.

Machines in which a paper roll is provided upon which a voter can write the names of those for whom he desires to vote, whose names do not appear upon the printed ballot, make it possible to write a key name, if two or more co-ordinate offices are to be voted for at large. This applies to any form of ballot, and any attempt to prevent it involves a contradiction or opens the door for cumulative voting. The only absolute solution is either to forbid independent voting or to permit every voter to file a complete list of candidates to be printed on the bollot. The first method might prove to be unconstitutional and the latter would be a practical absurdity.

The use of a paper roll for the independent vote, disassociated from the voting keys for regular candidates, while not theoretically perfect, appears to be the nearest practical solution of the subject.

In investigating and testing voting machines we have found two dangers to be guarded against : one, manipulation on the part of a voter to cause the machine to register more than such voter is entitled to ; and the other, manipulation on the part of the person charged with preparing the machine for an election, by which the returns may be falsified.

Machines which record all the votes cast by each individual by one movement, after or as the voter leaves the voting booth, are less liable to be tampered with by the voter than those which attempt to lock each key as the voter proceeds to cast his vote. The separate locking of each voting device, as used, is open to the objection that it prevents a voter from correcting a mistake, while those which operate all the registering devices by one motion, only record the used keys as left by the voter and hence afford no temptation or possibility for repeating.

The danger of manipulation of the machinery on the part of the persons charged with preparing the machines for an election is not so easily guarded against in the design and construction of the machine, but to meet this difficulty we would suggest, in case the legislature adopts a machine which provides for the arrangement of candidates in groups for one office, that : '' As soon as the period for recording nominations by parties and by petition is closed, all machines to be used in the ensuing election shall be examined and put into order by expert officers, to be appointed by the Board of Election Commissioners ; and the counting mechanism placed at zero. The machines shall then be locked and sealed so as to prevent any access to the working parts. Ten days before the holding of an election the name of each candidate for the same office or co-ordinate offices shall be written on a separate piece of paper, which shall be folded so that the name written thereon cannot be seen or read without unfolding the same ; and when the names are so written and folded they shall be placed in a box to be provided for the purpose and thoroughly shaken. The Board of Election Commissioners shall then open said box in the presence of a majority of said Board and in the presence of such members of the various political parties as may be present to witness the same, and shall then take from said box such slips of paper and the names thus drawn for each group of candidates shall be placed upon the machines in the order in which they are taken from the box. If a machine with party columns is adopted, the columns could be drawn for in like manner. By the adoption of this method all temptation to prepare a counting mechanism so as to favor or injure the record of a candidate would be removed and all danger of the manipulation of the machine by those charged with preparing same for an election would be eliminated. This method would also remove the objection to the present alphabetical arrangement of names on the ballot, which tends to favor candidates whose names commence with the early letters of the alphabet.

Special provisions to fit the construction of any voting machine which may be authorized by the legislature will have to be substituted for the detailed instructions governing election boards now incorporated in the election laws of the State, but no radical change in the methods of conducting elections will be required in substituting the machine for the ballot. It will be advisable to retain Section 1210 of Art. II. (Appendix " C ") so modified as to furnish instructions to voters how to use machines for voting and furnish them with a fac-simile of the ballot as placed on the machines.

By the use of machines it will be possible to avoid such crudities as are involved in Sec. 1255, Art. II, which reads, in part: "The ballots must be immediately replaced in the box and if the ballots in the box exceed in number the names on the lists, one of the judges must publicly and without looking in the box, draw out therefrom singly and destroy, unopened, a number of ballots equal to such excess."

Under this provision no voter is certain that his vote will be counted—the ballot of an honest elector may be cancelled and the fraudulent one retained. The mere casting of a ballot does not insure its being counted or, if canvassed, that it will be read off correctly. In a properly designed machine every vote cast will be correctly counted and no more votes can be cast than the total number of voters taking part in the election.

We have examined in detail the following inventions:

J. G. SWEENEY, San Francisco, Cal.

His system consists of tally sheets enclosed in a case with glass top and sides. In each case there are four tally sheets arranged in two columns, each column occupying half the length of the case. Two of the tally sheets are attached to each of a double set of rollers, which operate to move the tally sheets one voting space for each voter. The names of all regularly nominated candidates are printed in columns and are fixed on one side and in the middle of the case, so that when the tally sheets, which are ruled in parallel lines the length of such sheets, are moved, the spaces between such lines come opposite the names of the candidates, Slots are cut in the glass top of the case so that an X can be stamped upon the tally sheet opposite the candidates for whom a voter may desire to vote, and all the X's thus stamped appear in line. If a voter desire to vote for a person whose name is not printed upon the ballot he can write the name upon the tally sheet crosswise through the slot. As each voter completes stamping the tally sheet and leaves the booth, an election officer moves a handle outside the booth, which moves the part of the tally sheet used by the voter out of sight and rings a bell to indicate that the act has been completed. The unused portion of the tally sheet, for a space of about six inches, is always in view of the voters, through the glass top of the case, so that if any X's were stamped upon the tally sheet in advance of the election, such action would be open to detection. For an election two or more of such cases are used in each precinct and at the close of the polls all of the tally sheets are taken from the cases and are placed in a square basket, where they are so shaken that the identity of each is lost and all knowledge of the continuity of the voters who have used them is destroyed. Each tally list is then placed back into the cases and passed under the open slots for inspection so as to discover whether any voter has exceeded the number of votes to which he was entitled. If such be found the election officers stamp such excess X's with a circle, thus: (X) After all the tally sheets have been inspected they are taken from the cases and are separately placed upon a table and the number of X's—(X) omitted—for each candidate are counted and the total set down at the right end of the sheet. After such count is completed the tally sheets, which are lettered AA. BB, etc., to correspond with a like lettering upon the section of the ballot appearing upon the top of the machine, are placed in juxtaposition to their respective sections of the ballot, and not until then is the count for each candidate disclosed.

This system would save the printing, numbering and binding of ballots, the services of ballot-clerks on an election board, and would obviate the misreading of ballots, either by accident or design, as well as the mistakes which, under the present system, are possible in marking the tally sheets. In other words, the voter would record his wishes directly upon the tally sheet without the intervention of ballots and officials. The size of the machine is not objectionable and the system can be mechanically carried out in a simple and satisfactory manner.

The system does not, however, overcome one objection to the present ballot system: i. e., the identifying the act of a voter by writing a key name in independent voting. As all the X's of one voter appear in line when the tally sheet is being inspected, a given name written upon the tally sheet through the slot, will disclose the voter to any one in the secret who has access to the inspection. The use of a lever in charge of an election officer to move the tally sheet forward, while immediately protected by the sound of a bell, would in practice become liable to abuse, as the sounding of bells for two or more machines would in time become confusing and in such a case a voter might purposely be permitted to repeat his vote. No one officer could be held responsible for an excess of votes as no one officer could be expected to operate the lever during the entire length of an election. Furthermore, it would be possible to manipulate the bell in the machine so that it would strike but once, even if a privileged voter had used a number of voting spaces.

Any device which permits a voter to repeat his vote while in the voting booth is liable to abuse and cannot be too carefully guarded against. Such devices should be automatic and not be dependent upon the honesty or watchfulness of an election officer.

J. B. TERRILL, Newark, Cal.

This system consists of a number of boxes enclosing rollers upon which tally sheets are placed so as to move from one roller to another as they are used. Above the rollers there is a perforated sheet to correspond with the voting squares of an Australian ballot, and above this is placed a regular Australian ballot with strips cut out which otherwise would be occupied by voting squares. The perforations in the lower sheet are in juxtaposition to the names of the candidates and blank spaces on the ticket and there are a set of rollers for each column.

To vote, the voter opens a box and marks upon the tally sheet through the perforation opposite the name printed upon the ticket. To vote independently, a name has to be written upon a special ballot and deposited in a ballot box provided for the purpose. After marking the tally sheet the voter closes the box and thereby moves the tally sheet a voting space out of sight of the next voter. At the close of the polls the tally sheets are taken from the boxes (a number of which are used in each precinct) and the count is made directly of the marks upon them.

————

To eliminate illegal votes each tally sheet would have to be inspected and the excess of votes cancelled. Under this system there would be no check upon a voter marking the tally sheet and voting on the special ballot. Any possible gains would be offset by greater disadvantages than at present exist.

————

HENRY H. NIEBUR, Ferndale, Cal.

His system provides for a paper ballot, a ballot holder, a counting machine and a ballot box; the ballot is printed in party columns at right angles to the offices to be filled, with a column of blank spaces in which a voter can write the name of any person not printed on the ballot. To the right of the name of each candidate there is a blank square in which a cross could be stamped in case the other fixtures connected with his system were destroyed. The ballot-holder (a number of which can be in use at once) consists of a hinged frame, the underside of which is perforated to correspond with the voting squares on the ballot and the upper side is provided with receptacles to contain a single metalic ball immediately above such perforations. One end of the ballot is affixed to a spindle and is then placed within the ballot holder so that the voting squares will come between the receptacles for the balls and the perforated spaces below. For every office to be filled there is a column of receptacles which are filled with balls. The ballot thus placed in the ballot holder is given to a voter who takes it to a voting booth and transfers the balls, by means of a magnet, to such receptecles as he may desire (in place of stamping the ballot as at present) and he can change the balls from place to place untill he finally leaves them as he desires, thus obviating calling for a new ballot to correct a mistake. The ballot holder which is then covered to conceal the acts of the voter, is handed by the voter to an officer who places it in the Counting Machine.

This machine is arranged in compartments to hold the balls cast for each candidate. A frame with teeth to enter each voting receptacle in the ballot holder is mechanically pressed down so as to force the balls in the receptacles through the ballot into the compartments below, thus recording the vote cast and making a hole in the ballot in place of stamping it. The ballot is then wound up on the spindle, removed and placed in the ballot box. At the close of the election the contents of each compartment in the counting machine are separately drawn off by the removal of a slide bottom and the contents run into a scaled tube which at once shows how many votes were cast for each candidate. The total number of balls cast for each office plus any unused balls should equal the number of voters taking part in the election. If by accident or design more balls should appear, recourse would have to be made to the ballots in the ballot box in order to detect the source of excess. The inventor claims for his system the advantage—"That his machine during an election is always in charge and control of the Board of Election Officers—the voter not having any access or control over it, but voting as now by an Australian ballot."

A machine constructed upon the above principles to accommodate a fixed number of political parties could not be used in an election, if an additional number of candidates in excess of such provision should be nominated, and the whole system would break down. Evil disposed persons could bring any number of balls into the voting booth and thus destroy the utility of the counting devices. To canvass the independent vote, all the ballots would have to be opened and examined. Either by accident or design the operation of the ball counting devices could be overcome and resort to canvassing the ballots be necessitated. Instead of X's, as under the present system, the holes made in the paper by the balls forced through the ballot, would have to be inspected and counted. The complications proposed in this system offer no advantages over the present system.

———

C. L. STURGES, Escondido, Cal.

His system consists of an Australian ballot, a Counting Machine and a Ballot Box.

To vote, a voter uses a pointed instrument with which to puncture the ballot, instead of stamping an X. The voter then inserts the ballot in the Counting Machine, which permits metal balls to pass through the holes made in the ballot and collects them in scaled grooves provided for the purpose. At the close of an election the accumulated balls in each groove disclose the vote cast for each candidate.

The Counting Machine counts for all holes made in the ballot, so that if a voter should make two or more holes for, say, a Mayor, all would be counted. As a consequence, all the ballots would have to be taken from the ballot box in which they have been deposited after passing through the Counting Machine and be canvassed for the independent vote and for the purpose of eliminating illegal votes.

The system differs from the present, in substituting holes for X's and the trouble of passing the ballots through a Counting Machine without accomplishing a correct count.

———

AMERICAN BALLOT COMPANY.
McTamany Patent.
Mass.

This system comprises a Voting Machine proper, a Counting Machine and a Ballot-box, and affords a voter the option of voting entirely by machine or by ballot. The Machine, which is arranged for party columns, does not limit the number of candidates for whom a voter can vote, as he can vote upon it for every candidate nominated, but makes it impossible to vote for the same candidate more than once. The Counting Machine is depended upon to cancel the votes cast in excess. For example : If a voter should vote for two or more candidates for Mayor none of the votes would count. In case a voter desires to vote independently for any one he has to vote by ballot for all candidates for whom he desires to vote. The results of the two systems are added together and the total vote for each candidate obtained.

The Voting Machine is operated by push buttons which cut holes in a paper strung between rollers, which moves a given distance for each voter. In case of possession of the poll list and the punched paper, the act of each voter can be determined. The Voting Machine is mechanically well constructed and simple in operation. The Counting Machine is very complicated and delicate, and would require a watchmaker's skill to repair.

Under the above system, unless the present ballot system was also maintained, the door would be opened to place prepared ballots in the hands of voters which could afterwards be identified, and the voters would also be obliged to cast their votes under more burdensome conditions than those using the machines. As a consequence, the cost of the machines and their operation would have to be added to the present expenses incident to an election.

CALIFORNIA VOTING MACHINE COMPANY.

Christ Christensen, Patent No. 534,494.

This machine is operated by turning the exposed end of a screwrod upon which a nut with an index point moves one thread for each complete revolution, and indicates upon an accompanying scale the number of votes given to each candidate. A rod with gravity sliding blocks limits the time a voter can vote for a single or co-ordinate office, and as the voter leaves the booth these blocks fall together and leave no clue as to how the voter exercised his choice. The act of leaving the booth also completes the revolution of all the screwrods which a voter has partially turned. The voter is thus afforded an opportunity of changing or correcting his votes until he has left the booth.

For each office or group of offices an attachment for independent voting by ballot is provided, which, if used, prevents the voter from operating any rods for the regularly nominated candidates for that office. Where co-ordinate offices are to be filled, this arrangement necessitates the writing the names of regularly nominated candidates for whom the voter may desire to vote as well as those not nominated—all on one ballot in order to avoid cumulative voting. Such a ballot could readily be identified by an agreed name written upon it and would facilitate fraud in the purchase of votes. As each voter would be entitled to a ballot, however provided or regulated, it can be readily seen that such a ballot could be taken unused · from the voting booth and prepared on the outside and given to a subsequent voter, and thus an endless chain of corrupt votes could be controlled.

To the record of the vote shown by the nuts, the count of the ballot would have to be added before the total vote for each candidate could be known.

By coupling machines together any number of offices and candidates can be provided for, but in case of an excessive number of candidates for a co-ordinate office, such as the election of 18 Supervisors in San Francisco (which might result in over 100 candidates being nominated) a special machine to be used horizontally and provided with slide blocks operated otherwise than by gravity would have to be constructed, as a perpendicular machine controlled by gravity slide blocks would be too high for practical use.

The machine exhibited is mechanically well constructed, simple in design, and difficult, if not impossible, to get out of order.

UNITED STATES BALLOT BOX.

Franklin Grove, Illinois.

This system consists of a box enclosing a nest of vertical tubes, so arranged as to receive metal discs dropped into them. Above the tubes is a metal plate in which slots are cut, through which such discs can pass. A second plate composed of metal strips with corresponding slots in them, rests upon the bottom plate, so that the slots in both will admit of a disc falling through them into the tubes when all are brought together. The slots are so arranged that candidates can be grouped with party columns at right angles to the offices to be filled, and the box can be constructed to accommodate any reasonable number of candidates for an office. The names of candidates need not necessarily appear in party columns.

In voting, a voter opens the cover to the box and places a disc in a slot opposite the printed name of the candidate for whom he desires to vote, and in so doing forces the metal strip sideways into such a position that a second disc cannot be placed in any other slot in the same strip. The disc, however, can be withdrawn and placed in any slot in the strip as long as the box remains open.

To vote independently, there is a lid in each metal strip which can be raised provided the voter has not deposited a disc in the same strip, exposing a paper roll upon which he can write the name of a person for whom he desires to vote. The raising of the lid moves the metal strip in the same manner as placing a disc, but a lid once raised the metal strip cannot be again moved so that a voter can place a disc in a slot. All the names written by one voter appear in line and cumulative voting can thus be detected if practiced.

The voter having arranged the discs for the candidates for whom he desires to vote, the lid to the box is closed and a crank is actuated which carries both the metal strips and bottom plate into line over the mouth of the tubes so as to drop the discs into them. A continuation of the movement restores the sliding strips to their normal position, moves the independent roll one voting space, if it has been used, and closes the raised lids so as to obliterate all traces of the acts of the voter.

At the commencement of an election a flat metal rod is inserted into each tube so as to demonstrate that all are equally empty, and at the close of the election the same process is repeated and the votes cast for each candidate are disclosed by the depth to which the scaled rod will descend.

In case of co-ordinate officers to be elected at large, it

would be impossible to vote for more than one candidate appearing upon the same strip. To overcome this defect it is proposed to allow the voter to write upon the independent roll the name of a candidate whose name appears printed upon the strip, for whom he cannot insert a disc. This method, however, would also make it possible for a voter to vote for the same candidate twice; i. e., once by disc and once on the roll.

Unless these difficulties can be overcome this device would be practically useless.

The mechanism used in this device is very simple and positive and only a tension spring to control the paper roll is used. The cost of construction would consequently be moderate.

The use of discs preserves in a concrete form the record of each vote cast. In case of dispute the box can be brought into Court for examination and the discs cast for each candidate be either measured, counted or weighed. In this respect the system differs from those employing registering wheels, where the count is abstracted in the position of the wheels and the individual acts of the voters are obliterated so as not to be subject to review.

F. X. ST. LOUIS, Elk Creek, California.

His machine is arranged so as to receive a lineal ballot. Opposite the name of each candidate there is a sliding key, in one end of which is a receptacle for a disc. To vote, a disc with a hole in its center is inserted in the above mentioned receptacle and the key moved forward so as to draw the disc under a plate and over a vertical rod upon which it drops. A sliding device prevents two or more keys being moved forward at the same time. Teethed wheels in which stops are placed, limit the number of times a voter can vote for either single or co-ordinate offices. A lever controlled by a turn-stile or the officers of an election board, releases the used keys after each voter has occupied the voting booth. The machine can be adjusted to meet the conditions of succeeding elections and can be made to accommodate any number of candidates. To vote independently, one key is reserved in each group of single and co-ordinate offices. For this purpose discs upon which a name can be written are furnished the voters. So far as single offices are concerned this method could be adopted, but for co-ordinate offices various complications arise. Except by experts in hand-writing, no one could tell whether eighteen voters had each voted once for one supervisor or one voter had voted eighteen times for the same person. A machine which might accommodate all the independent votes for mayor, might prove incapable of holding all the independent votes for eighteen supervisors to be elected at large, as all would have to be dropped on one rod. If eighteen rods were provided for voting for independent candidates for supervisors, cumulative voting might be practiced without detection.

At the close of an election the rods are exposed with the discs which have been dropped upon them and a scale discloses the number of votes which each candidate has received. The independent vote has to be canvassed separately.

So far as the principles involved in this system for voting for regularly nominated candidates are concerned, they could be carried out with mechanical accuracy. A voter can see that his disc drops upon the rod in line with the candidate for whom he is voting, and before moving the sliding key, he can change or correct his vote.

HENRY WEBER.   Patent No. 531,818.

Temescal, California.

This Voting Machine is designed to receive a lineal ballot. Opposite the names and blank spaces are receptacles in which discs can be placed for those candidates who are selected by a voter. Such discs can be re-arranged until the voter has prepared his vote to his satisfaction. Slide-blocks limit the number of times a voter can vote for single or co-ordinate offices and these can be adjusted to meet the requirement of succeeding elections.

To vote independently, the voter is permitted to write a name upon a disc. For the purpose of casting his vote, the voter removes a block which operates to cover the receptacles for discs and permits those in position to fall into scaled tubes.

Until the machine is adjusted to receive another voter, no more votes can be cast. At the close of an election the number of discs in each tube discloses the number of votes cast for each candidate.

Counting by this device could be accomplished with certainty. The arrangement for independent voting is defective as cumulative voting could be practiced and escape detection. The position of the slideblocks, as left by each voter, would indicate how such votes had been cast.

————

S. A. CUMRINE, Los Angeles, California.

This system consists of a line of voting keys set opposite the names of candidates. To vote, a voter turns a key a quarter turn, which actuates a toothed disc one tooth and cannot be further moved until a releasing bar in charge of the Election Board prepares the way for a subsequent voter. In case of single offices the movement of one key locks all the others for the same office, but for co-ordinate offices where, say, two out of four candidates are to be elected, each voter could vote all the four keys unless prevented by the Election Board, who would have to keep tally by ear as each key was operated. The system contemplates separate machines for each office or group of offices to be filled. For independent voting, keys in excess of those to be used for regularly nominated candidates are provided with a blank space opposite in which a voter can write the name of a person for whom he desires to vote. In practice, three candidates for mayor might be regularly nominated and keys provided for them, but to accommodate a possible independent vote, ten, twenty, fifty or more keys and blank spaces would have to be provided, as no one could determine in advance how many independent votes might be cast.

At the commencement of an election all the discs should be found at zero, and at its close the number of votes cast for each candidate could be read off without difficulty.

STANDARD VOTING MACHINE COMPANY.

Gillespie Patent.

New York.

This machine is arranged with eight perpendicular party columns and a column for independent voting, at right angles to the offices to be filled. In addition there are placed at the foot of the machines eight spaces for the submission of questions, constitutional amendments, etc., for which a key can be placed in position to vote yes or no. A system of interlocking wedges limits the times a voter can vote for a single or co-ordinate office, and the machine can be adjusted to meet the conditions of succeeding elections to the extent of a full list of nominations by eight parties. The mechanical principles involved in the interlocking system do not advantageously permit of an increase in the party columns, but the number of offices to be filled can be increased in the construction of the machine to meet the requirements of any election. A perpendicular paper roll to the right of the party column affords an opportunity to write a name not printed in the party column, by moving a slide over the paper, but a slide once opened prevents a voter moving any of the voting keys in the same line. As the perpendicular roll moves forward but once for each voter using it, any attempt at cumulative voting can be detected.

The machine permits of the grouping of eighteen supervisors to be elected at large and can, therefore, accommodate the names of 144 candidates and eighteen spaces in which the names of those not nominated can be written. The interlocking system and a special device will prevent a voter placing more than eighteen keys in position for voting. The voter can select his candidates at will, unless he chooses to vote for a line of candidates running across the bottom of the group so as to vote for several from each political party. In this case the angles of the interlocking wedges do not permit all the keys being placed in position for voting, and also prevent a free choice of candidates above the bottom line. If certain keys were used it would be impossible to vote for a certain 79 out of the 144 candidates. To the left of the names of the various candidates is a column of voting keys, which in the act of arranging his ticket, a voter moves at an angle over the name of the candidate of his choice. All the keys in one column can be moved into position by the use of a lever at the top, but after using such lever, if a voter desires to split his ticket he can move back any or all of the keys singly and move a key in any other column over the name he wishes to vote for or vote on the independent roll.

Upon entering the voting stand the voter moves a lever from left to right, which carries a curtain in a semi-circle in front of the machine and encloses him in the booth. He can then arrange and re-arrange in secret the voting keys for the candidates of his choice, which being accomplished, he returns the curtain lever to its original position and in so doing registers his vote, and the movement of the lever restores the voting keys to their normal position and closes the slides over the independent voting roll. When not in possession of a voter, the face of the machine is exposed to view of all present and any tampering with it can be readily preceived and the blame be promptly placed. At the commencement of an election the registers in the back of the machine are exposed for inspection and all should be found at zero. The rear doors are then locked and cannot be opened while the voting keys can be moved. At the close of the election the voting keys are locked, the rear doors opened and the registers show the number of votes cast for each candidate. The independent roll has to be canvassed separately.

The use of voting levers (which can either be retained or discarded) at the top of each party column expedites voting without limiting the number of offices for which a voter can vote, nor confining his choice to party candidates, and would enable a greater number of voters to use a machine in an election than if each voting key had to be separately placed in position. The question naturally arises whether the use of such levers would conflict with the decision of the Supreme Court in Eaton vs. Brown.

The printing of the names of regularly nominated candidates upon the ballot, as now provided by law, saves time and effort and enables the class of voters who place an X opposite such printed names an advantage over those who are obliged to write the names of those for whom they desire to vote and the principle of "more burdensome conditions" is not carried to *reductio ad absurdum*. A corresponding practical construction of the law would doubtless permit of the use of a lever for the purpose of facilitating the arrangement of the keys for voting.

This machine is thoroughly adapted for an election in which the number of candidates for a single office does not exceed eight and for co-ordinate offices forty (five only to be elected), but any increase in the number of candidates for a single office or for a group in excess of five to be elected for co-ordinate offices, is beyond the mechanical limits of the interlocking mechanism of the machine. These difficulties can only be overcome by the adoption of a new interlocking device or by a law raising the percentage required for a position upon the ballot and limiting the number of officers to be elected at large to five.

The machine is finely constructed and is easily adjusted to meet the requirements of succeeding elections; all the movements are positive and only a tension spring for the paper roll is used. In operation any voter is capable of comprehending it and can adjust the voting keys with ease and rapidity. Up to its capacity elections would be conducted with it at an economy in cost and certainty in correct results.

NATIONAL VOTING MACHINE.
Markøe Patent.

This machine is arranged in sections which are set one upon the top of another. Each section is complete in itself and can be coupled with others for the purpose of releasing knobs which have been used in voting. The face of each section exposes a line of voting knobs so arranged that each can be used for voting for a single office or combined for voting for a single and for co-ordinate offices, so that any number of candidates can be accommodated. The knobs, to each of which a ridged pointer is attached, are placed in the center of a slotted receptacle, and from each slot a space radiates in which the name of a candidate can be placed, with or without a party designation. In the machine exhibited eight such radiating spaces appear, but their number could be increased. For independent voting there is an opening in the top space over each knob and all these openings are in line. Separate rolls of paper pass before such openings, but all are attached to a common shaft and move forward once whenever a voter elects to write the name of one or more persons whose names are not regularly printed, so that cumulative voting cannot be accomplished without detection.

In order to vote the voter turns a knob so as to bring the pointer opposite the slot and space on which the name of the candidate appears for whom he desires to vote and then pushes the knob inward. A knob thus pushed cannot be withdrawn, but at once actuates the register counters and completes the act of voting. A mistake in placing the voting pointer into a slot cannot, consequently, be recalled and corrected. The vote for each office is a repetition of the above described method. When the knob is pushed inward against the independent space a slide opens and exposes the paper roll, which at all other times is covered. After a voter leaves the voting booth a lever, which can be operated by turnstile or the election officers, throws all the used knobs outward, dropping the pointer into its normal position and closing all the slides which have been opened for independent voting. At the beginning of an election all the registers, which are exposed upon the back of the machine, should be found at zero, and upon opening the machine at the close of the election, such registers will show the vote cast for each candidate.

For the purpose of releasing and returning the voting knobs to their normal position a shaft extends the length of each section, which could be reached by an opening made and concealed in the outside casing. By means of a wire reaching the shaft through such opening, a reciprocal action could be set up which would permit of a voter voting for one candidate an unlimited number of times. While such a fraud might be known by the general result, it could not be located even though the opening in the casing was found, as the shaft operates all knobs alike. This defect could probably be overcome by some device which would retain the releasing bar in a fixed position while a voter was in the voting booth, but as the machine is now designed it could be pumped in the manner indicated.

In the case of presidential electors this machine affords the voter the option of voting for a straight party group by one movement, or of voting for such candidates separately, and the interlocking device will not permit of both methods being used by the same voter. This method involves the adding together of the straight party vote and the votes cast for candidates separately in order to obtain the total cast for each. It enables, however, a greater number of voters to use the machine in a given precinct and in consequence is economical in the number of machines required for an election and the number of election officers to be employed.

J. C. GARREET.
San Francisco, Cal.

Presented an incompleted model of a Voting Machine, but as the device was only partially disclosed it is impossible to give a satisfactory description of it.

H. A. CLIFFORD.
San Francisco, Cal.

This device consists of a bank of numbered voting keys placed above an Australian ballot. To vote, a voter pushes inward a key corresponding to the number placed opposite the name of a candidate on the ballot, thereby locking the mechanism so that another vote for the same office cannot be cast. For co-ordinate offices the machine can be adjusted for any number of candidates. To vote independently, the voter pushes a key for a blank space and thereby raises a lid upon which he can write the name of a candidate whose name does not appear upon the ballot. A double system of recording the vote is provided by the use of a paper roll and registering wheels. The push keys are connected with double arms, one of which punches the paper roll, which serves as a tally sheet, and the other actuates registering wheels. All movements are positive.

The interlocking device consists of a series of wedges passing between hanging rods which permit of a free passage until the limit of candidates to be voted for single or co-ordinate offices has been reached. The interlocking device of the machine exhibited permits of twelve candidates to be elected at large to be chosen out of fifty. A special device will permit of only a portion of the offices to be filled to be voted for in case such an arrangement is desired. This machine provides for cumulative voting as allowed in some states.

ELLIS BALLOT MACHINE COMPANY.

Livermore, Cal.

In this machine a ballot arranged the same as the present one would be if the names of all the candidates were printed in one column, is placed opposite a row of voting keys which extend the length of the machine. The ballot is folded so as to expose to the voter the names of the candidates and blank spaces for independent voting. The reverse side of the folded ballot, which is reserved in columns of hundreds, tens and units, for the result of the election to be printed thereon, is placed over registering wheels which are in line with the push keys. The names of the candidates and the blank spaces on the ballot are thus placed immediately above the registering wheels, which are actuated by the voting key opposite such names and blank spaces.

By a system of gravity balls placed in double rows the number of times a voter can push down the keys to vote for single and co-ordinate offices is limited to his legal right and can readily be adjusted to meet the conditions of succeeding elections. While in the voting booth, a voter, by pulling up a depressed key, can correct or change his vote as often as he chooses, and is not confined to any fixed order of voting, but can choose or change his candidates at will.

For independent voting a paper roll extends the length of the machine and passes over a supporting table. By pushing down a key opposite the blank for independent voting, a lid is raised over the paper roll, upon which a voter can write the name of the person for whom he desires to vote. A lid once raised its key cannot be returned to its normal condition until the voter leaves the voting booth, nor will pushing down other independent keys by the same voter advance the voting roll. If a voter writes the same name more than once such names will appear in line and detect his act the same as if the present ballot was used. A voter can thus vote for such regularly nominated candidates as he may choose, and vote for anyone he may desire not nominated until his limit of voting is exhausted.

Upon the voter leaving the voting booth, the independent roll, if it has been used, is moved forward one voting space, the independent lids close and the depressed keys are released and resume their normal position, thus removing all trace of the acts of the voter. At the same time the registering wheels, which at all other times are securely locked, are moved forward for such keys as have been left pushed down by the voter and his vote thereby registered.

At the opening of the polls a regularly prepared ballot, such as is to be used in the election, is inserted in the machine, the lid closed and locked and an impress of the registering wheel printed upon the ballot. This impress should show that all the registering wheels are placed at zero. The ballot for the election is then inserted and is protected during the election by a transparent covering. At the close of the election the lid of the machine is again closed, an imprint taken upon the actual ballot used, showing the changed position of the registering wheels which have recorded the acts of the voters and consequently the result of the election so far as the votes for regularly nominated candidates are concerned.

By opening the lids over the independent or scattering vote and turning the roll backward, such votes can be canvassed without removing the roll from the machine, and the total of such scattering votes cannot exceed the number indicated by the imprints on the ballot opposite each voting space. A turn-stile, provided with a conspicuous moving arm and a gong bell, unlocks and locks the Voting Machine as each voter enters and leaves the voting booth, so that

without the knowledge of all present it would be impossible
for a voter to vote more than once or for a vote to fail _of_
being registered.
Sections of this machine, which can be made of 50, 75
or 100 keys, can be coupled together so as to accommodate as
many parties and candidates as may be desired.

This device meets many of the requirements of a practical
Voting Machine, and complies with all the provisions of the
Election Laws of this State, save the option of voting for a
group of Presidential electors instead of voting for such candidates separately.

CHRIST CHRISTENSEN, Oakland, Cal.

This machine is enclosed in a narrow upright box. In
order to vote, a voter passes to one side of the box, which is
placed in full view of all present, and raises a cover which is
hinged together, so that when the cover is raised it acts as a
screen. The machine is then operated by the voter raising a
screw-rod and inserting a resting-arm attached thereto within
a notch of a slide-bar which extends the length of the machine.
Upon the screw-rod (which is numbered upon the rod for each
half-turn) there is a movable nut (protected by a guide rod)
which moves upon the screw-rod as the latter is turned. The
names of the various candidates to be voted for appear in
groups the same as if the existing ballot was printed in one
column and these groups can be so changed as to meet the
requirements of succeeding elections. This lineal ballot is
placed upon the top of the machine so that the name of each
candidate and the spaces for independent voting appear opposite the handle to a screw-rod. A system of rollers and
wedges at the bottom of the screw-rods limits the number of
screw-rods which can be raised by each voter and the times a
voter can vote for a single or co-ordinate office. The same
device permits the voter to correct or change his vote as often
and as long as he remains in the voting booth, and he is not
confined to any fixed order of voting but chooses his candidates at will.

For independent voting a paper roll feeding from one to a second roller extends the length of the machine and passes over a fixed table. This table is covered by arms which can be attached to each screw-rod, but for an election only those arms are attached to the screw-rod which are reserved for independent voting. To vote independently, the voter raises the screw-rod and inserts the resting-arm within the notch of the slide-bar, thereby lifting the arm over the fixed table and exposing a space upon the paper roll upon which he can write the name of anyone not printed upon the ballot for whom he desires to vote. In this operation the paper roll is moved but once, no matter how many times the voter may write the names of independent candidates, and as a consequence all the independent votes of any one voter must appear in line upon the paper roll. This cannot prevent cumulative voting, but detects it in the same manner as the present ballot does, and while it discloses the act of a voter it does not identify him. The voter can thus exercise the limit to which he is entitled by raising the screw-rods and voting for candidates regularly nominated and those of his own choice and is only called upon to write the names of the latter. After once raising the screw-rod for an independent vote the rod cannot be replaced by the voter in its original position, as otherwise he could write upon the roll and afterwards vote for regularly nominated candidates the full number of times permitted. After the voter has arranged the screw-rods in the notches in the sliding-bar, he closes the cover to the box and thereby moves a cam operating the sliding-bar, which moves all the resting arms forward until they are released and fall back by gravitation into their normal position, thus completing the half revolution of the screw-rods for independent as well as regular candidates, and forcing the nut to register the vote given and removing all traces of the acts of the voter. The cover to the box cannot be closed until all these operations have taken place. Any attempt on the part of a voter to open the cover a second time to repeat his vote would be apparent to all present and such attempt should open the doors of the penitentiary to him.

At the commencement of an election the machine can be opened so that spectators can see that all the nuts are placed at zero in the machine and at its close the result can be read from the rods as shown by the position of the nuts. The independent vote can be canvassed without removing the paper roll from the machine as it can be turned back space by space and the names read off through an opening provided for the purpose. During an election the only parts of the machine which could be tampered with (which are the resting-arms and slide-bar) are exposed to view by means of a glass cover ing, and any possible injury to them could be seen by every voter. The movement of the nut upon the screw-rod is absolutely positive and the nut cannot be moved a half turn unless it has been operated by the act of a voter—the numbers appearing upon the screw-rod itself, in the same manner as upon the balance arm of a weighing scale, does not permit any tampering with or manipulation, and as the movement of the operating cam only permits of a forward motion when the resting arms are in the notch of the slide-bar, a vote once registered cannot be set back and cancelled. In these respects the design is unimpeachable.

Machines in sections of 50, 75 or 100 keys can be coupled together so as to accommodate any number of parties and candidates. One hundred or more candidates can be grouped together for single or co-ordinate offices and the mechanism does not limit the number of co-ordinate offices to be filled. Thus, the voter could select one candidate out of a hundred for Mayor and eighteen out of any hundred candidates for Supervisor to be elected at large.

By the use of a special device a straight party group of presidential electors can be voted for on one rod, so as to afford a voter the option of voting for such group by one rod or of voting for the same or other candidates separately, and the interlocking device will prevent the use of both methods by the same voter.

If this method of voting for a straight party group to fill co-ordinate positions could be lawfully extended so as to permit a voter to vote, say, for eighteen supervisors to be elected at large, the interlocking device of this machine could be adjusted to meet the requirement. This would facilitate rapidity in voting and a far greater number of voters could use a machine than if each candidate had to be selected and voted for separately.

This group method would involve the adding together of the straight party vote to those cast separately.

A screw-rod is mechanically equivalent to a pile of connected discs and the passage of a nut upon it accomplishes the same purpose as placing one disc upon another. Hence, the recording mechanism in this machine combines both the concrete and abstract features which distinguished the disc and registering wheel machines.

This machine meets all the requirements of a practical voting machine, and complies with all the provisions of the Election Laws of this state.

It has been our purpose in examining machines to study the principles rather than the execution of the devices, as most of the machines presented have been imperfectly constructed. In a machine manufactured for practical use, many existing minor faults could and would be corrected. The "McTammany" and "Standard" machines illustrate how well machines can be manufactured. Of the hand-made machines, the "National," the "Ellis" and the "Christensen" are the only ones which have been made upon a scale to admit of practical tests. In general principles they are somewhat alike, though the mechanical devices are entirely different, and each possess advantages which have already been mentioned. The "Ellis" is the most compact and the "Christensen" the strongest and least complicated.

It was the intention of the commission to give public exhibitions of the practical workings of Voting Machines submitted to us for examination and testing, but we have to regret that delays upon the part of inventors in completing their machines has rendered it impossible for us to make such tests in public.

Whatever machines may be adopted, it will be necessary to enact laws guarding them against being marked, defaced or injured and to prevent the use of devices to disclose the acts of a voter who might be placed in the voting line between two conspirators. To guard against such practices the booths should be arranged so as to expose the voting keys to public view before each voter proceeds to vote.

As previously stated, the " McTammany " and "Standard " are the only factory-made machines, all the others having been made by hand and exhibit variation in workmanship from crude models in wood to finished products in metal. As a consequence it is difficult to make an estimate of the probable cost of one or more of such machines. The price for factory-made machines would doubtless range from two hundred and fifty to five hundred dollars.

An important factor in the economy of voting by machines is the number of voters who can use a machine during an election. Machines which require each key to be separately moved cannot accommodate as many voters as those which place a party group into position for voting by one movement. At the last election held in Rochester, N. Y., on November 8th, 1898, seventy-three " Standard " Voting Machines were used, sixty-two candidates were in nomination, thirtern positions were voted for and an average of four hundred and thirty-one voters used a machine in each precinct. Complete returns were received at a central station thirty-seven minutes after the close of the polls. Under the newly adopted charter of San Francisco, thirty-two positions will have to be voted for at each election, and as under the existing law each candidate must be voted for separately, the number of voters who can use a machine in a precinct will be less than the average in the late election in Rochester.

By the use of machines the cost of conducting an election would be reduced by the expense for ballots and the lessened number of election officers employed. Doubtless it would prove advisable to retain an inspector, a judge, two register clerks and two poll list clerks. As their services would be required for only a short time after the close of the polls, a reduction in the amount now paid them could be made—thus : in San Francisco where twelve election officers are employed in each precinct at a cost of ten dollars each, the savings in expenses for officers, ballots, tally-sheets, etc., would soon cover the cost of machines.

The moral gain in the avoidance of mistakes and the certainty of the count would prove of inestimable value, and would far outweigh all minor considerations.

W. M. HINTON,
C. B. MORGAN,
J. V. WEBSTER.

APPENDICES

APPENDIX "A."

An act to create a commission for the purpose of examining, testing and investigating Voting Machines, and reporting to the Legislature at its thirty-third session the result of such investigation, and making an appropriation for the expenses of such commission.

(Approved March 27. 1897.)

The People of the State of California, represented in Senate and Assembly, do enact as follows :

SECTION 1.   A special commission of three persons is hereby created for the purpose of examining, investigating and testing Voting Machines, and reporting the result of such examination, investigation and test, together with the opinion of such commission, and its recommendations, to the Legislature at its thirty-third session.   Such commission shall consist of three persons, who shall not be members of the same political party, to be appointed by the Governor.   The Governor shall issue a commission to each of the three commissioners.

SEC. 2.   Such commissioners shall receive no salary for the performance of their official duties.   Immediately after such commissioners shall have been appointed, or elected, and commissioned, they shall meet together, and organize, for the performance of the duties for which they were appointed or elected.   They shall examine and investigate all Voting Machines offered for such examination, or investigation, and shall use all reasonable efforts to secure a personal examination of the largest possible number of such Voting Machines. They shall endeavor to ascertain the names and residences of the patentees, owners, or proprietors, of all such Voting Machines, and by correspondence, or by advertisement, notify them of the appointment of such a commission, its powers and duties, and that they will examine such machine or machines, at such time, and at such place, as they shall therein specify.

Sec. 3. They shall be allowed to employ a clerk at a cost not to exceed six hundred dollars, and may incur such other expenses as shall be necessary, which, together with the expense for such clerk, shall not aggregate more than one thousand dollars.

Sec. 4. Thirty days before the meeting of the Legislature at its thirty-third session, such commission shall forward to each member of such Legislature entitled to sit at such session, a copy of its report. Such report shall contain the results of their investigation and examination; their opinion upon each machine tested; its applicability to our present elective system, and its possible defects. Such commission shall also in such report make such estimate as may be possible and they deem proper of the probable cost of one or more of such machines, and the saving, if any, which such purchase would effect over our present system of voting.

Sec. 5. The sum of one thousand dollars is hereby appropriated out of any moneys in the state treasury not otherwise appropriated, for the purposes of this act, to be expended by such commission, as herein provided. All claims against this appropriation must be presented to, and allowed by the State Board of Examiners.

Sec. 6. This act shall take effect immediately.

APPENDIX "B".

Oakland, Cal., July 3, 1897.

Hon. Wm. F. Fitzgerald,
Attorney-General of California,
San Francisco.

Dear Sir:

As a member and as acting secretary of the commission created by act of the last Legislature of California for the purpose of examining, testing and investigating Voting Machines, and under authority of a resolution passed at the last regular meeting of the commission, I write to you in your official capacity to learn your interpretation of the entire act, and more especially of the following portion, viz: "its applicability to our present elective system and its possible defects." Some of the machines offered for our inspection are apparently very perfect and highly successful in operation, and meet all the requirements of the election laws, excepting only that part of Sec. 1196, Pol. Code of California, reading as follows: viz: "Nothing in this Code contained shall prevent any voter from writing upon his ballot the name of any person for whom he desires to vote for any office, and such vote shall be counted the same as if printed upon the ballot, and marked as voted for." Is this a mere legislative enactment, or is it also a necessity under the constitution?

Is our commission bound by the existing law, or can we recommend changes that seem to us wise and advisable?

Trusting that you will render us your valuable opinion as to these matters, I am,

Yours truly,

(Signed) C. B. MORGAN, Sec'y.

California Voting Machine Commission.

———

"APPENDIX "B".

REPLY TO FOREGOING.

ATTORNEY-GENERAL'S OFFICE }
STATE OF CALIFORNIA. }

W. F. FITZGERALD, Attorney-General.

San Francisco, July 7, 1897.

California Voting Machine Commission,

Room 507 Central Bank Building, Oakland, Cal.

GENTLEMEN :

I am in receipt of your favor of the 3rd inst. in which you request my "interpretation" of "An Act to create a commission for the purpose of examining, testing and investigating Voting Machines," etc,, "and more especially to the following portions, viz: "its applicability to our present elective system and its possible defects."

The act in question (Stats. 1897, 222–223) creates a commission "for the purpose of examining, investigating and testing Voting Machines, and reporting the result of such examination, investigation and test, together with the opinion of such commission and its recommendations to the Legislature at its thirty-third session."

(SEC. 1, Stats. 1897, 222). By section 2 of the Act it is provided that the commission "shall examine and investigate *all* Voting Machines offered for such examination, or investigation, and shall use all reasonable efforts to secure a personal examination of the largest possible number of such Voting Machines." Section 4 of the Act relates to the report of the commission, and contains the following provisions, in which occurs the phrase upon which you particularly request my opinion :

" Such report shall contain the results of their investigation and examination ; their opinion upon each machine tested ; its applicability to our present elective system, and its possible defects. Such commission shall also in such report make such estimates as may be possible and they may deem proper of the probable cost of one or more of such machines, and the saving, if any, which such purchase would effect over our present system of voting."

In reply to your question : " Is our commission bound by the existing law, or can we recommend changes that seem to us wise and advisable ? " I am of the opinion that it was the purpose of the Legislature in framing the Act creating your commission to obtain, through you, all the information possible concerning Voting Machines, their feasibility, cost and cost of operation, etc. ; and that it is the duty of your commission to examine all machines presented to you for examination or that you can obtain the privilege of examining and to report fully to the Legislature upon each machine so examined, its merits and its defects, and its applicability or non-applicability to our existing laws governing elections ; and I am further of the opinion that you are not in any way restricted by the Act in the matter of recommendations ; but that you were expressly created for " the purpose of examining, investigating and testing Voting Machines, and reporting the result of such examination, investigation and test, together with your ' opinion ' and your ' recommendations,' to the Legislature at the thirty-third session." The Legisla-

ture desires the fullest information for its guidance in consid-
ering its feasibility of adopting Voting Machines, and one important element of such information is the change which it
will be necessary to make in our present elective system should
such machines be adopted.

Respectfully,

(Signed) W. F. FITZGERALD,

Attorney-General.

REPLY TO THE ABOVE.

Oakland, Cal., July 10, 1897.

HON. W. F. FITZGERALD,

Attorney-General of California,

San Francisco.

DEAR SIR:—Your reply of July 7th to our letter of the
3d inst. is received, and its contents are carefully noted.
The question which we wish to have solved is "whether a
voter has a constitutional right to vote independently, i. e.,
for a person who has received no nomination by any political
party; or whether such right exists by virtue of a mere
Legislative enactment ?"

To construct a Voting Machine which would register an
independent vote, would add much to its complication and
expense, and lessen many advantages.

Yours respectfully,

(Signed) C. B. MORGAN, Secretary.

California Voting Machine Commission.

REPLY TO ABOVE.

San Francisco, July 30, 1897.

CALIFORNIA VOTING MACHINE COMMISSION,

Central Bank Building, Oakland, Cal.

GENTLEMEN:—I am in receipt of your favor of the 10th
inst. in which you ask, "whether a voter has a constitutional
right to vote independently, i. e., for a person who has received

no nomination by any political party; or whether such right exists by virtue of a mere Legislative enactment?''

This is an extremely delicate constitutional question and one which is not necessary for me at this time to pass upon, as an opinion thereon by me would serve no practical purpose. All that is required of you, under the Act, creating your Commission, is to examine Voting Machines and to report to the Legislature their feasibility, and their adaptability or inadaptability to the existing laws concerning the elective franchise, their cost, etc., accompanying your report with such recommendations as you may see fit to make. If you have any doubts as to the constitutionality of any changes in the law which you may recommend to meet the exigencies of either or any of the machines reported upon you can so state; and it will be for the Legislature to determine whether or not, in view of the constitutional questions involved, it will adopt such recommendations.

Respectfully,

(Signed) W. F. FITZGERALD,
Attorney-General.

APPENDIX "C."

ARTICLE II. SECTION 1210.

The County Clerk of each County, or, in case of separate city or town elections, the clerk or secretary of the Legislative body of such city or town, shall cause to be printed, on plain white paper, without water mark or endorsements (except the words ''Sample Ballot ''), at least as many copies of the form of ballot provided for use in each voting precinct as there shall be registered voters in such precinct. Such copy shall be designated "Sample Ballot," and shall be furnished to registered voters at the office of such clerk or secretary five days before the day fixed by law for such election, and at any time during such five days ; *provided*, that not more than one sample ballot shall be furnished to any one voter. Such clerk or secretary shall cause to be printed, in large clear type, on cards, instructions for the guidance of electors in obtaining and marking their ballots. He shall furnish twelve such cards to the Board of Election in each election precinct in his county, at the same time and in the same manner as the printed ballots and sample ballots. The Board of Election shall post at least one of such cards in each booth or compartment, provided for the preparation of ballots, and not less than three of such cards at other places in and about the polling-place, on the day of election. Sections 1214 and 1215 of this Code and Section 61 of the Penal Code, shall also be printed on each of said cards,

www.ingramcontent.com/pod-product-compliance
Lightning Source LLC
Chambersburg PA
CBHW021556270326
41931CB00009B/1244